Who Me? I Can't Sell A Darn Thing!
Learning the basics of how the industry works

BJ Stephens

Copyright © 2012 BJ Stephens

All rights reserved.

ISBN:197944529X
ISBN-13: 978-1979445290

DEDICATION

This book is dedicated to all entrepreneurs everywhere. It takes massive courage to follow your dreams, hopes and desires and even more courage to pursue your passion in spite of all the naysayers you will encounter. It's also dedicated to those who believe in themselves and have a strong desire to make something better for their future and their families future. It takes a strong will to go after what you want and not lose focus in spite of those many days where you second doubt yourself and wonder what you got yourself into, and my friend, you will have them. What matters is surrounding yourself with only those who will support you, guide, love and push you through those brick walls and help you achieve all that you hope to dream.

I believe that everyone has extensive value, importance, and worth and we spend a great deal of our life wasting our time pursuing those things we *think* we want instead of pursuing was we are best suited for. This book, although it deals with sales and marketing, is actually dedicated to those who have a dream that sings to their soul and will make those sacrifices to learn through the failing process. Those who understand that there is no such thing as failure. Only learning experiences with each *time we try.* It is to these people that I proudly dedicate this book.

This book is a nudge in your direction. This is my effort to tell you I believe in you, I know that you can do this...because you have magic!

CONTENTS

	Acknowledgments	I
	In the beginning	
1	The 7 Basic Requirements to Sell Anything to Anyone	1
2	Develop Your Story – Facts Tell, Stories Sell	12
3	Show Your Customer the "WHY" and the "NEED"	17
4	Establish Your Knowledge and Expertise	21
5	Hurry! Time is Running Out To Make Your Purchase!	25
6	Free Gifts Are Your Best Marketing Tool	32
7	Commit Yourself In Every Way To Your Customer	36
8	How Do You Keep Your Customers Interested?	40
9	Understanding What You Can and Cannot Do	44
10	There's No Such Thing As Perfect But You Can Become Better By Failures	50
	BONUS: Invest In A Coach And Mentor – The Extreme Value	

In the beginning…

I would be extremely derelict in my purpose of this book if I didn't first mention right out of the gate that there are several things that must be taken into consideration before entering the world of entrepreneurism or a home based business. These things must be given great consideration before any final decision is made.

First, don't make any decision based on how attractive the offer is or based on how much money you are "promised". That is a sure fire way to fail from the get-go. As you are looking at opportunities prepare a set of questions that concern you the most; things like how much do I have to invest? (and yes, most opportunities require you to invest some kind of money. It is no different than starting a brick and mortar business. It requires capital to start a business of any kind so makes sure that you know how much you have to invest before you agree to any kind of commitment).

Prepare numerous questions that concern you and begin the "interview" process with the person who is trying to recruit you. Don't shy away from hard questions, make them answer wholly and in full detail. If you get any kind of evasive response then say thank you and move on to the next opportunity. Any time the person is hemming and hawing around then they either have not been trained well enough to act as your leader, they are only interested in your money or, worst case, they have no scruples, integrity or character and that is definitely NOT what you want to connect with. Make them do THEIR best to show them they are worthy of YOU. Even though you may have absolutely no experience whatsoever in whatever type of business you are pursuing, make that person do their utmost to show you what they are made of and how serious they are about working with you. This is absolutely critical to your success.

Research several companies, don't just go with the first one that "looks good". I can tell you, without question, there are some pretty slick people out there and they will be expert at answering those "typical" questions so make them work for your attention. Go with your gut…it never lies. If it really does sound too good to be true then yes, it probably is. Oh, and one more thing, if that person "guarantees" you anything, be skeptical, be very skeptical. This is a business with absolutely NO GUARANTEES because the results are entirely based on how good your training is, how much work YOU put into doing what is necessary, and how dedicated you are in becoming successful.

BJ STEPHENS

Bottom line, success isn't convenient; it requires sacrifices, focus, determination, willingness and gobs of work. There will be times you will question your decision...that's normal...it happens to even the most successful in the beginning. Remember even those who are earning mid six figure incomes or seven figure incomes all began where you are now. They too, had to go through the growing pains of starting their own business and you will as well. Having the right mindset and common sense when entering into this kind of profession will serve you many times over.

One of the other crucial things you need to to that most do not do in the beginning is you need to set your family down and have a conversation with them about what you are considering, why it is important and what it means to everyone involved. Discuss things like role changes (there will be times that another family member may have to assume an occasional chore or task that you used to do). Inform them that in order for this to work you will need to ask for their cooperation as well. Some members will have to step up to the plate and do more than they have been doing so that you can focus on whatever it is that will take up your time. This isn't all about you. Your family is just as involved and this is a conversation that, although may not be pleasant or easy, is an absolute MUST before you make

Also include in this conversation the amount of time, money, sacrifices that may have to take place. Discuss, for example, what will have to be done if you cannot bring in an income for several months (and yes, this may happen, but don't get discouraged!), what luxuries can you do without for a period of time so that you can focus on making your new business a success and get it off the ground. Ask all family members to take into consideration that what you ask of them now will hopefully benefit them in the future. You may want to share with them this is kind of like going back to college; it takes several years to complete that learning experience and this will be no different. Just make sure that you include them in the decision making, get their feedback, share with them your feelings and why you are doing this. I can tell you from decades of experience this is absolutely crucial for your mindset, your overall success because when you have the support of those around you it makes this journey so much comfortable, less stressful and makes it tons easier to handle.

There are several other things that go into the preparation you need to do before making a final decision. All I can strongly recommend is that you enter into this with your eyes wide opened, use common sense, don't allow anyone to push, intimidate or harass you into a decision that you don't feel right or comfortable with. Listen to your heart, head and gut before leaping. After all, this is your and your family's future we are talking about here and even though you make a misstep on occasion (and yes you will so don't worry about that), when you are armed with intelligent questions to launch your search with, chances are you will be much happier with your choice(s).

Here's to your success!

ACKNOWLEDGMENTS

Where in the world do I begin? This list is quite extensive and I fear that I will inadvertently leave someone out so with that being said please forgive me if I fail to list anyone here. It's not that you haven't been appreciated or loved, just regrettably overlooked.

The first place is to begin with those amazing mentors in the beginning who spirited me and gave me the encouragement to believe in myself and my abilities. My first time meeting the legend, **Zig Ziglar** gave me not only such enthusiasm and passion for sales but he appreciated the fact that the most important part of sales is the people themselves. Without them there would be no business, no sales, no paycheck. Even though he was a small statured man his voice was booming and not only grabbed your attention immediately, his southern drawl was charming to say the least.

Next comes the one man who put the "magic" into what I had chosen to do; the god-father of personal development, **Jim Rohn**. I loved this man immensely. To me, he was as wise as any sage of our area but he had such a "grandfatherly" presence" and tone of voice. Listening to a training of his was like sitting in your living room with your grandfather and he was sharing life lessons with me, common sense thinking, and he did so with such a gentle, non-judgmental voice. I 'm not joking when I say I loved this man. When he passed several years ago I grieved as hard as if he had been a blood relative of mine.

The third person who knock me out of my socks was another giant in his field; a man whose deep baritone voice and unique laughter melted my heart and gave me one of the most glorious moments of my life. This gentleman changed my entire vision, deepened my internal belief in myself and made me want to make him
proud. I speak of the one and only **Les Brown**, the number one motivational speaker in the entire world. It is through him that everything changed for me and gave me belief that I was indeed capable, deserving, and talented enough to follow in his footsteps and for that I will always be eternally grateful. Such a powerhouse!

Next comes another man who touches my very soul; with whom I connect in so many ways. I had always been a avid follower for so many years and have read just about every book he has written but when I "jumped" and decided to take my professionalism to the next level he was the one I sought out. I speak of the amazing **John Maxwell**. Here, also, is a man, who I give all credit for seeing something in me and pushing me to reach my very best.

WHO ME? I CAN'T SELL A DARN THING!

There are indeed so, so many others who have contributed to my success, who have worked so closely with me and behind me, who have pushed when I need the push, to scold when I needed that as well, but who mostly supported me beyond belief with their patience, love, tenderness and guidance. I hope you know who you are. You all have my undying gratitude for being there with me through thick and thin. Just to mention a few of my personal friends who have now and will always be a part of who I am: **Bill Ebert, Maria Ebert, Robert Hollis, Carrie Bradford, Dianne Law, Irene Doniger, Collette Wiedecke, John and Nadya Melton, John-Leslie Brown** and so many, many others to mention. No one will ever be a success without the support of many and I have indeed, been richly blessed many times over for such connections.

A HUGE appreciation and acknowledgment goes out to all my private and corporate clients. Thank you for believing in me and trusting me as your coach, trainer and mentor.

You are true angels on earth and I could not have done any of this or have been successful without your love, support and belief in me. Because of you I am rich beyond words!

1
THE 7 BASIC REQUIREMENT TO SELL ANYTHING

FOOD FOR THOUGHT:

Fear isn't a permanent life style. It can actually be your friend if you use the lessons it teaches to improve your future.
Use your fears to help you grow in knowledge, skills, wisdom, compassion, and to improve your life.

Ever heard the phrase, "People like to buy but hate to be sold". It's true. Think about your own personal experiences. Don't you just cringe when you are in a social setting and someone says something like "Hey, are you still interested in…? Call me this week because I think I can now be of assistance." If you are trying to sell something to someone and they feel your urgency you have just lost your sell, regardless of whether or not they like your product. There is a process that logically goes and flows in the sales world but few take the time to learn everything first. There really is a psychology of sorts that comes into play if you are to be remotely successful in sales. You need to develop and learn the basic concepts below to master the art of selling if you want to become successful. These concepts will be discussed in further detail later.

Key # 1 – Establishing the right Environment

I hate pushy sales people and I am sure you do as well. Take the time to build a relationship with your potential customer. You don't always have to start out with your pitch. Let them get to know you first. Take time to establish a friendship, a ***relationship***. It's called the "Know, Like and Trust" principle. Invite them to lunch, a cup of coffee or perhaps dessert. You might even consider offering a Skype or Zoom call so that you can actually have a visual contact and you both get an opportunity to put a voice to the meeting. Which ever way you choose it is important to establish that initial rapport, a connection, a friendship before pitching your product. Show a genuine interest in them; ask simple questions about them, their family, their occupation, their hopes, dreams, and desires. Ask them what it is that keeps them up at night. When you show a genuine interest they are much more willing to open up and share the answers that you will need to have down the road. If you set the sale up properly then the customer will be much more receptive and willing to listen to what it is that you do what it is that you have to offer.

Key # 2 – Making Your Product Seem Important

Once you have established that relationship (and this could take a few days or weeks – don't rush!), people won't buy things that aren't important to them or they feel that they just don't need at the moment. So, you need to advise them on your product's utility; it's benefits, features, and usefulness in their lives. Explaining how this product will enhance their lives, save them money; make life easier for them, etc. gets their attention but not necessarily the sale. Being able to show that this product is a necessity in their lives requires that you understand your clients' needs and that takes practice. Go all over town telling how undeniably useful your product is, and a lot more people will be interested in it. It may sound a bit old fashioned but public meetings are kind of like community infomercials. Talk to small groups, hold parties in your home or theirs, and seek out public meeting rooms that do not charge a fee (most public libraries will have meeting rooms that you can schedule an event in without charge). Ask other clients to offer their testimonies, use documented research on the product or its ingredients; use flyers, brochures, anything that will help you promote your product. Word of mouth is a potent ad campaign. The more others use and like your product the more you can reach others to understand how important this product is in their lives. This means you are building your business foundation; your reputation, your credibility. Once your name and your product is more widely known your customers and professional community will have no trouble endorsing you.

Key # 3 – Start Branding You

All right, so your product is useful, but why should they buy from you? Why are you better than the competition? You have to show your customers that. You have to tell them why you and your product are better for them than what the competitive market is selling. You must create integrity, confidence, honesty, reliability, and sincerity with that customer. Remember, if that one customer finds you responsible enough, reliable enough, trustworthy enough to do business with, they will pass that word on to family members, co-workers, neighbors, and those that they do business with. I cannot stress this enough, word of mouth is your best advertising in sales, bar none. Think back to a time when you were speaking to someone or a group of people about a bad experience or product. As you start sharing your experience someone speaks up and says something like, "Oh, HIM (Her)! I used them and had such a bad experience I will *NEVER* call them again." Even though that customer may have been a one in a thousand customer who wasn't satisfied, those few words will stick in the mind of the others present that day. That negativity has now just cast a shadow of caution and doubt about you and your product. People are like elephants…they do not forget.

Key # 4 – Establishing a Sense of Urgency

Remember that people want to buy but hate to be sold. You must create a sense of urgency in your delivery yet do not create an atmosphere of desperation. Let them know if this promotion is only for a limited time; advise them that this sales price goes away at the end of the month (or week or at the end of the day today); share with them that this opportunity is only for a short time and if they do not act right away it may cost them more if they procrastinate. Be perfectly honest with them. If the product is on sale at this moment for, let's say $10 but that price will go up to $20 at week's end, let them know that this kind of sale only happens twice a year. It would be a huge savings to them to act now. Inspire that sense of urgency in their purchase. "By buying now you are saving 50% off the retail price and it will be another six months or more before they offer this kind of savings again." This often brings in better sales believe it or not. Here's another fact: People love to think they are getting a bargain!

Key # 5 – Free Samples and Make Sure You Follow Up

Offering free items can often be the best marketing tool you have. It will cost you a few bucks but if the customer realizes that you do value their time and appreciate that they gave you a moment out of their day, it can create a long lasting relationship which can only ensure continued sales in the future. Just put yourself in their place. How often have you received something for free only to go back to that person or company and make a purchase down the road? It gets my attention every time.

Free samples also allow the customer to "test drive" the product before purchase. They may have some questions regarding its usefulness or purpose and a free sample is one sure way to introduce them to your product. Make sure you leave them your business card so that they can contact you if they have questions.

But just don't give them the product and leave it at that. **FOLLOW UP!** One of the first lessons I learned (in the hardest way possible) is that the *"money is in the follow-up"*. This is where most newbies (and a lot of professionals) make their biggest mistake. When I was selling Avon decades ago, I called upon a woman who was getting married within the next couple of months and she was looking for gifts to give to her six brides maids and others who were in the wedding party. I spent about thirty minutes with her and got a feel for some of the things she was interested in. Before I left I gave her some samples of our newest product, some cologne samples along with some personal care items. Since she also was considering gifts for the groomsmen as well I left samples of things I thought might appeal to them as well. I felt really good about our meeting and knew in my heart that she was going to be making a purchase. I left behind my business card and her last words were, "I will take a look and talk it over with my fiancé. Once we decide which items we want I will give you a call". I got in the car and felt on cloud nine because I knew the chances of her placing a very large order was high. So I waited, and waited and waited for her call. Three weeks went by and no call so I dropped by one afternoon to see if she had made a decision. Indeed, she had. Because I had not bothered to follow-up with her quickly she contacted another representative and placed an order for what I found out later to be over $500!! Of course I was devastated but I learned a very valuable lesson that day. Just because they tell you they will call you doesn't mean they will. I wasn't considerate enough to understand that she had a lot going on at that time in her life and I should have put myself out there to make it easier for her, not wait around for her to make my sale for me. What a doofus I was! Because I waited for the customer to come to me I lost out on over $150 in commission! So listen to me when I say call them, email them, or drop by in a few days to see if they like the product. Don't wait around. A good rule of thumb is to get back with them in 3-4 days. This is where many customers are lost because people are busy these days and it is just easier for you to contact them than waiting for them to get back with you. Always, always, always follow up!

Key # 6 – Committing Yourself to Your Customer

Make these people understand that you will be there for them even after you have sold the product. This gives them a guarantee but you had better be prepared to honor that promise! Customers **HATE** salespeople who do not live up to their expectations. Let them know that if they need to replace or send back their purchase that you will gladly do so without question. No hassles, no delays. You are going to offer them the best customer service that you can provide them. A very good piece of advise here: fully understand what your company's return/exchange/replacement/money back policy is and commit it to memory. Know it forward and backwards before you have to deal with this issue. In fact, it can and should be used as a sales tool. If customers know upfront that they have, let's say, a 100% money back guarantee, then you put them at ease and will feel more comfortable knowing that if they need to return the product they can do so with peace of mind. Never forget that this is *YOUR* business and if you fail to honor your word you have just lost sales…period. Also remember that thing about word of mouth? Yep, it works REALLY well when you have upset a customer because now they are angry and will tell the world about you and how you do business. This can ruin you fast!

Key # 7 – You've Got the Customer's, Now What?

Now that you have your customer base how do you keep them shopping with you? Here is where you need to give them value in exchange for their purchasing month after month. The sky is the limit and you just need to use your creativity here. Show them you are as committed to them as they have been to you. Appreciation is needed by all of us whether we are customers or employees. We all need to feel that what we do matters to others. Put yourself in their shoes and think back to someone you did business with, an insurance agent, an electrician, a contractor, etc. Did you get upset or frustrated when you felt that they were taking advantage of you? Did they leave out part of the job? Did they do sloppy work? Were they hard to get ahold of? Did you feel that you were not a priority with them? C'mon, admit it, you have more than likely said something to the affect, "I'm paying them good money and look how they treat me? If that's how they feel about my business, then I won't be back." Right? Yes you have. Your customers are no different.

Back to my story about my bride-to-be. If I had been on my toes, I should have not only contacted her quicker but I should have gone out of my way and done something special for the bride, like a bride's basket made up of full size bottles of personal care items, jewelry, cologne, etc. A gift basket of sorts and made that my gift to her as a thank you for her sending her business my way. I should have shown some appreciation.

Do right by them and they will keep coming. Treat your customers the very same way you want to be treated by those you do business with. You not only will have very happy and satisfied customers you will have customers for a long time and your checking account will thank you too.

2
DEVELOP YOUR STORY – FACTS TELL, STORIES SELL

FOOD FOR THOUGHT:

Everyone loves stories. Only, adults love stories that have emotions and ring true.

A wise marketer will use and perfect this craft to become a true professional

It is a highly competitive world we live in without question. It is the unique, the different that attracts our attention these days. No body likes the ordinary, the cookie cutter, same ol', same ol'. In order to stand out from the rest of your competitors you need to create your brand, that one thing that will bring you and your product to the first thought of your customers.

What better way to get noticed right out of the gate than a great story? We aren't talking about becoming a Mark Twain here. However, this is not a story about how you came up in the business, not is it how this business brought

you such great wealth. This story is about YOU and how it

relates to the needs, concerns and issues of the people you are speaking to at the moment. For example, if you are speaking to a newly divorced mom of three who is desperately seeking a solution to meeting net months rent payment, car payment, or perhaps something so simple as putting dinner on the table this evening, don't begin by telling her that you have the best company where she can make a lot of money in the next few weeks or months. Don't tell her that your products/service will solve all her problems. Instead, share a story of how you can relate to her *feelings, concerns, show compassion to her emotional need* by sharing something similar that you experienced personally or maybe even a family member or a friend. RELATE! EMPATHIZE! Talk about how difficult it is to give her kids the basic necessities. Talk about how much you worried about tomorrow when you didn't have a clue what tomorrow would bring. That kind of story. It is part of building that relationship; that know, like and trust thing I spoke about earlier. If that person gets the feeling that you are sympathetic to their deepest worries and fears then you will make a great relationship stronger. It's the sharing of the emotion that is a strong bond. If you do not have a personal story that relates with your customer's pain points or needs then share a story (a brief one!) of an acquaintance or of a friend's. Don't discount the power of the story just because you don't have one that relates.

Don't think that you don't have a story. Everyone has. You just have to dig it out and don't worry that it doesn't sound professional. In fact, the more authentic and personal it is the better. Was there some obstacle that you kept confronting? Perhaps you almost never made it because you kept running into one obstacle after another. That's a story. Or maybe you got a single jolt of inspiration that suddenly put the idea of possibility in your head. That's another great idea for a story. Or you could give one example – and this would be to your great advantage –of someone who helped you, coached you or mentored you through the tough times and because of their assistance you finally took steps to begin on a new journey which has made all the difference in your life. Maybe you could even get a testimonial from them with their picture and signature and put it on your handouts or on your online sales page. Such things do work wonderfully; there's no question about that.

Testimonials are also stories and they can be extremely powerful to use however, be very cautious here. Remember, at this point in your relationship you should not have even started a conversation about your business. Don't leap the gorge before you or they are ready. Once you have made that leap now use the testimonies for confirmation about how good your product/services are or how joining your business has had a huge impact on their lives. The major plus point about testimonials is that someone else says them and hence they strike a better chord with the readers. In any case, stories work, whether they are your own or your users' testimonials.

But remember that the language of the story is very important. Put passion into your story and, don't forget, to be true and honest. People have a sixth sense to insincerity and will lose interest immediately if they feel you are wasting their time. Just like a good story written in a bad style does not appeal to anyone, a story told in a voice that sounds contrite, made up and outrageous will lose you customers in a heart beat. Get real. Put meaning in your story. You should probably practice with a recorder just to make sure that you sound authentic. It is truly all in the delivery and by ensuring that your voice's pitches, tone, emphasis on strong words are hitting the mark with you, chances are they will with your customer.

You could get a great professional writer from GetAFreelancer or ScriptLance to write up a good story for you. You give them the idea and they make a human-interest tale out of it! I am not a huge fan of this method for several reasons but if you feel that it may help you then by all means invest the effort. I tend to be a bit old fashioned. If I cannot communicate effectively and with passion about what I personally believe in, then my customer isn't going to get very passionate about my product or me. Right?

Believe it or not everyone has a story to share and it does make you relatable and authentic to your customers. It really does help the sale when your customers know what you have experienced in the past and have overcome.

In the media world they say, "The sale is in the story!"

3
SHOW YOUR CUSTOMER THE "WHY" AND THE "NEED"

Food for thought:

Stop to think about what makes you want to go out and purchase items.

Is it need?

Is it desire?

Is it value?

Is it because your best friend has it?

Is it because it will make your life better?

WHATEVER THE REASON ALWAYS PUT YOURSELF IN YOUR CUSTOMER'S SHOES. UNDERSTAND WHAT MAKES THEM WANT TO BUY AND CREATE THAT ENVIRONMENT

WHO ME? I CAN'T SELL A DARN THING!

People don't purchase things on a whim in today's world. Everyone has become quite conscious about money, especially because of the recent economic problems that the world has seen. But it is still a good time to start business. No fooling. People have money, but they are simply more cautious about spending it. The frivolous spending habits of people that we saw just a few years ago have toned down drastically. But people are people, they will start spending frivolously again, but until then you have to make them see why they should buy something from you. (Remember, people want to buy but now you have to show them why).

You can do this by making people understand why they should buy your product, and that becomes your second requirement of making successful sales.

Whatever your sales pitch is – the sales page, a television commercial, a magazine or a newspaper advertisement – the focus should be on what the product can do for the people. You have to tell them what benefits they can get out of them and the more succinct you are about those benefits, the better it will be. Let people know what their money will give them.

When people are convinced that they are spending their money on something useful, they won't mind spending the money. It should be something that spells real utility to them.

You must know that people don't see things that you don't tell them. Now, you might be selling a steam iron, but until and unless you actually outline the advantages of getting a steam iron, people won't think of buying. People won't buy it just because it exists or because you tell them it is a good deal. However, if you could make a bulleted list of its benefits and advertise that on your sales page or even in the mall where it is sold, you will find people buying it. You can actually hear people saying things like, "Hey, this so much lighter and look at this. It's got a lot more steam holes than that other model. And look at this, I don't use nearly as much water to get steam" and you can say, "You bet and it makes your ironing go so much faster. Now you can get a more professional look with your items. Who wants to be ironing all day?"

See what I mean? People talk themselves into buying things when the benefits of it are outlined. They almost convince themselves to make the purchase. Yes, it does mean that sometimes you may have to do a product demonstration but sometimes people just have to see the benefits with their own eyes.

Don't be afraid to let them touch, taste, feel, smell, hold, or whatever it is that they want to do. It is just like that old adage, "Proof is in the pudding".

4
ESTABLISH YOUR KNOWLEDGE AND EXPERTISE

Food for thought:

Experience is always the best teacher. Why?

BECAUSE THE MORE YOU KNOW, THE MORE YOU EXPERIENCE, THE MORE YOU PUT FORTH THE EFFORT, THE MORE YOUR WISDOM SHINES BRIGHTER AND YOU BECOME MORE CREDIBLE TO THOSE AROUND YOU.

This is actually where your actual sales expertise comes into play. Making a list of the benefits is actually one of the most common things to do. Everyone who makes a sales pitch for his or her product will do that. But what you have to achieve is how you can make it special so that your people can't resist purchasing it.

One of the best ways to do that is to focus on how you and your product are better than the competition.

In a way, you have started on this already, right in the first requirement when you wrote your story, your personal testimony. You are stamping your uniqueness at that point itself. But now you have to put that forth in a more relatable way. Make them see what's so special about you. Speak of your special expertise in the area. Perhaps you were previously a teacher, a writer, a party planner, a public speaker, a nurse, a hairdresser, a make up artist, etc. What is your particular expertise that puts your stamp on this product? Speak why you are better than the others – maybe it is the creativeness of your product or an added feature that makes it unique or maybe even your better support system. Making actual comparisons with the competitor is always a good way to support your claims.

Be as transparent as possible in your relationships with not only your customers but with those you meet in public as well. Let others see the authentic you, the trustworthy, honest, reliable and down-to-earth you. Don't ever pretend to be something that you are not. Avoid trying to emulate your ideal salesperson. It won't work. When others see that you represent you and not some kind of pretend you, you will score big points with them.

Use forums and blogs to sell yourself. If you don't have a blog yet, I can recommend an outstanding format and company and one that uses WordPress. For more information visit my website at http://www.bjstephens.com and click on the tab at the top of the page that says "Make $ Blogging". There are tens of thousands out there today earning a substantial income writing blogs.

People can then interact with you and you with them. It is

a great way to get support and to get answers on questions that may pop up from time to time. They understand you are for real and that you have answers to their apprehensions. They get more convinced about you as a person. They don't mind buying from you. A great forum of professionals to start out with is WarriorForum.com. Get familiar with how it works and it can be a great resource for you, especially if you are new to the selling profession.

The best thing is that this helps you to rise above your competition. In today's competitive market, this is the most important thing you can do to enhance your products' selling prospects.

5
HURRY! TIME IS RUNNING OUT TO MAKE YOUR PURCHASE!

Food for thought:

As human beings we have a strong desire to want bigger, newer, better last week. We sacrifice, at times, our sound judgment and common sense in order to obtain what we think we need; the latest version of the hottest product.

The art of selling is recognizing our customer's desire to purchase and providing them that opportunity but also giving them value so that they feel they made the right decisions. All you have left to do is seal the deal.

How many times have you said, "I hate watching TV shows! There are more advertisements than show! I get so tired of watching all that crap!" Well guess what? There is good news and bad news. The bad news is I do not see those ads going away anytime soon. The good news is that as annoying as they may be, they work. If those ads didn't create a sense of urgency from you to buy, our free enterprise system would crumble along with our economy. Corporations and small businesses alike use advertisement because they get customers in the door or to their web page. Think about it. Would you want to spend money on something that showed no return on your investment? Of course not.

A great ad for a great product for a great price will end with "This offer is only for the next 3 days. Hurry!" The smiling blonde on the TV will demonstrate a product that you absolutely want (or think you want) for your home and then say, "These prices are good only until the boss returns from vacation!" or something stupid like that. Even the nerdy geek who puts his picture on the sales page creates an Armageddon scenario by stating that his prices have been dropped from $127 to $27 only for the next 24 hours. The truth is probably that his product was never anywhere above $27. Why? Mark-up baby! That is how businesses turn a profit. They buy at "x" dollars, figure out how much to reasonably charge without scaring the customers away, and they will usually fix that amount at a price so that when the item goes "on sale" they can still turn a profit. That is how business has been transacted for centuries.

But when you tell people that they are getting a bargain, they are always interested, even if the price after the bargain is more than the original price of the product elsewhere. Take gas for an example. The neighborhood convenient store is offering gas at ten cents a gallon more than the bigger corporate stations Why? Probably because the bigger stations can buy more bulk purchases and usually these days those bigger stations are affiliated with convenient stores. They actually make more profit off what the customer buys once they are inside, like soda, coffee, snacks, fast food, etc. Those smaller stations have to have a higher mark-up just to turn a profit so their prices will be a bit more expensive. However, some people will forego the extra expense for the convenience. They would prefer to pay the higher price and drive only two blocks than drive eight blocks for a few dollars in savings. Humans are sticklers for bagging steals because it panders our ego to understand that we have got a bargain. We love to feel like we have saved money. For example, imagine that you are shopping for a new car. Your dream car is, let's say, an Audi. You know you cannot afford that but you cannot help yourself and you arrive at the dealer "just to take a look". The salesperson asks a few questions and learns that you are just shopping however, during the conversation he informs you that they have a brand new finance plan that makes owning this vehicle now more affordable for people like you. Bingo! He struck a cord with your ego. Now you are thinking, "Wow! I can own this vehicle if I am willing to put $5000 down and pay $600 a month for the next 7 years!" Your common sense goes out the window and your desire just came to the head of the class. Even though you know that $600 a month is way over your budget you talk yourself into reasoning that you can go without cable/satellite TV for the next 7 years, or that you can stop eating out or going out with friends on the weekend. You try to justify the expense to satisfy your desire. BOOM! Done deal! After the first payment now you wonder what the heck were you thinking! I'm a raving lunatic!

It's called impulse buying and if you have never purchased an item because you just had to have it then call me. I have stock on planet Mars I would like to share with you. We all do it!

What really improves a bargain situation is the sense of urgency. The feeling of get-your-credit-card-right-out-of-your-wallet-and-buy-this-schmuck is what gets them every time. Of course, when you know there's just 36 minutes to buy something at half price, you will probably buy it. Even if that thing isn't useful to you right now, you will justify yourself by saying, "If I have to buy this tomorrow, I will have to pay a lot more." Chances are that you will buy that thing and then wonder why when reality hits and Doomsday arrives. A very good example of this is QVC. Now this company is expert at this technique and God bless them for their mastery! First they offer cookware at a special "featured price" and then throw in free shipping. They show the retail price then their price. Wow! Look at that! That's $45 cheaper! But hurry! This price goes away at midnight! Guess what? Now they have sold 1500 items during a 5-minute presentation. BOOM! Gotcha! And oh boy, you only have to pay six easy payments of $125! But wait, they're not done. The next item up is a very special ten-piece utensil set just made to work with your new cookware. Well of course, you got to have that, right? BOOM! You have now spent hundreds of dollars on your credit card that will charge you 18% or more interest and you ended up paying an extra $100 in interest to get "that special discounted cookware and utensil set". They created a beautiful sense of urgency and you were sold! It works folks and it will always continue to work. It is the psychology of marketing and it will remain with us until the last man on earth is standing. I love it! Master this and the world is yours for the taking!

But there's no reason why you shouldn't use this gimmick as well, considering that even the big name malls and supermarkets are putting ads for their hourly discounted sales. Remember, people love to buy and if you promote your offers well, you will get a good number of buyers. Don't try and act like a slick car salesperson though. Customers are much more wiser now than ever.

However, there are a few rules:-

- Your product needs to be good. Crap products means many returns which means you are not making a profit.
- The bargain has to be attractive. If you just knock 50 cents off your price, it isn't going to mean anything. Give your customers a discount that has value.
- The time you give them should be short but meaningful. Do not spend time with the tire kickers. If they are just browsing then move on to others who are serious shoppers.
- At the same time, the time shouldn't be so short that they think your offer is a scam. People want to feel a connection with the salesperson; someone who is paying attention to the fact that they may be spending money on their product. Remember people have become much more discerning now and will ask more questions about you and the product. That's okay. In fact, that is encouraging. It shows interest and never run away from interest. Return the favor and show interest right back.

6
FREE GIFTS ARE YOUR BEST MARKETING TOOL

Food for thought:

To your customers free is always a sign of appreciation.

"Give unto others and so shall you also receive". This is a truth as old as time and when applied to salesmanship it's gold.

But do not always think of this is terms of sales and developing a client list. Get active in your community and give back what they have given to you. Pay it forward by showing your support to groups and services that interest you.

When you give away things for free through your on line sales page, classified ads, brochures, or wherever you are promoting your stuff from, you are doing several things that directly benefit your prospecting game.

1. You are giving people a sampling of your quality. If your gift is really good, people somehow think that the real thing will be good too.
2. You begin a channel of communication with your people. Because you have given them something for free, the ice is already broken. You could now start making these people interested in other things.

3. You stamp your credibility. People understand that you really have some products that are probably made well too.

4. But the most important thing is that you are sending them on an emotional trip. Giving something away is as good as telling them, "You took something from me for free. Now, it is your turn to pay back by actually buying something." If the person was thinking about whom to buy a particular thing from, they will think about buying it from you just because you gave them something for free earlier.

When online marketers build their lists, they use this trick most often. They set up a blog and give away an eBook or a subscription to a newsletter for free. (If you follow my blog then you will know that I have done something similar to this in marketing my recent book). In return, they ask people for their email addresses. This becomes their list which they starting tapping into. They send emails to this list about their products and state their offers if they have any. When people are convinced about the quality of their product, they are very likely to make purchases from them.

Give people things for free, but don't do it without maintaining records of to whom you have given things to. That would break the communication forever. Even if they want to get back to you, they might not have bookmarked your site and will not know where to find you. So, remind people to bookmark your site or direct them to your blog, Facebook, Twitter, Pinterest account or any other social media page so that they know where you are. From there they can private message you and keep in touch. Most importantly, keep them on your list and keep promoting your stuff to them.

It also doesn't hurt to continue to offer "freebies" to regular customers from time to time, but be careful about using this strategy. Your goal here is to make a profit and if you give away more than you actually sell then you will be out of business in a heartbeat. Use this strategy wisely. A good example would be if you had a faithful customer who makes continues purchases month after month, year after year, and you become aware of a special event in their life, like a remarkable anniversary, or a major life achievement, or a birth or graduation, and so forth. To show your appreciation you might consider putting together a special package for them that contains their favorite products along with some other items that compliments your product. You don't have to go Martha Stewart here, just make it pleasing and thoughtful. You will score big points with them, believe me.

7
COMMIT YOURSELF IN EVERY WAY TO YOUR CUSTOMER

Food for thought:

Your customer is your livelihood. Without them you would be out of business, therefore, commit yourself to them in product, customer service, return policies, friendship, fair pricing, returning phone calls without delays, will all reap huge rewards for you and your business. Give value in all that you do.

People who want to buy from you want to make sure that you will be there for them. They want to see your commitment. No one likes fly-by purchases in which they buy something and then lose all contact with the seller. This might work if you are selling something for a dollar, but for most things that people buy today, they want to see the seller remain involved even after the sale has been done.

There is reason for that. They want to make sure that if anything goes wrong with the product, there is some remedy for that. Only the seller can ensure such a remedy. That is the reason people are promising so many money-back guarantees on the Internet today. Take a look at a sales page on the Internet – any sales page – and you will find that there is almost always a money-back guarantee. Sometimes these guarantees extend to up to 90 days. This is the period in which customers are free to buy the product, use it and check whether they will work for them or not.

You must also provide a good money-back guarantee. It should be of an ample time so that people are convinced that could nicely check the product and return it if they are not satisfied with it.

Most likely, they will never return your product. People are already very discerning when they buy and if you make everything quite clear on your sales page, they will know exactly what to expect. Be honest there, and you will have no returns of your sold products.

But what people want more than the money-back guarantee is a support system that continues after the product has been purchased. Most people aren't technical-minded and if your product requires the customer to use some kind of technical knowledge, you have to be there to guide them. You have to promise your unstinting support even after the purchase is done. Make sure your customer has a convenient way to contact you and make doubly sure that you return their call as soon as you possibly can. The longer the delay the impression of a bigger concern and that will give your customer the impression that you don't want to deal with them or their issues. Not good for you, the company or your customer.

Be honest and upfront about these promises and deliver them. This ensures long term selling prospects for your business.

8
HOW DO YOU KEEP YOUR CUSTOMER INTERESTED?

Food for thought:
In the beginning sales will be sparse because they do not know you however, once they become repeat customers never take it for granted they will stay your customer.
Develop a style that is uniquely yours that keeps them hooked and wanting to come back over and over again

Don't expect a lot of sales in the very beginning. Remember that you are establishing your customer base, your brand, your expertise and knowledge base. In the online world Capture pages'/Landing pages or your website conversions will happen but they will be very slow. In the offline world, it is much more likely that you will have some guaranteed purchases when people walk into your meeting or drop by your sales booth or table at a business fair, but even so when it comes to making a lot of sales know that you will have to put forth the effort to get others to notice you and your product. It is all about the exposure and how often you execute that exposure.

So, now that you have established your customer base you have to think about how to keep them coming back. Don't ever assume that a one-time purchase will keep them your customer forever. The one most important thing you must do is to keep the interest factor alive. It is for people like the tire kickers – you know the ones, those who want to browse or think things over a very long time - the drifters you might want to call them. The are the people who hesitate in their purchases and whom will help you build your future lists. These people might purchase, but they want that push to do so. When you have them on the list, you could keep promoting to them through emails, flyers, brochures or newsletters. Remember that you shouldn't send them such material without their expressed opt-in permission because if you do so, you become a spammer, and there's no dirtier tag than that when you are trying to do something on the Internet. Again, think about how much you hate those obtrusive emails that you never solicited that arrive in your email or junk folder daily. Because I follow a lot of companies or advertising you cannot believe how many spammers end up in my email. I discovered a very long time ago it is much easier and a lot less of a headache to just delete them when they arrive. Quick and easy, boom, it's done, until the next time.

Send them quality material. Send them stuff that will really interest them. Do your homework and learn what drives the particular niche you are in. They might want to know more about how-to stuff, DIY stuff, or maybe some tips and figures will interest them. Whatever it is they want to know, keep giving them such stuff at regular intervals.

The idea is to keep them hooked on. These people may have become interested in what you are trying to sell when they first visited you, but now they might be losing interest. When one of your 'meaningful' emails comes into their inbox, their dwindling interest gets a shot in the arm.

If things are going too long, you might even consider inviting them to download another eBook or sign up for another newsletter subscription for free. It works. Probably you could get another marketer to giveaway things with you. Such collaboration works in mutual interest.

People who are selling offline could also do this by announcing offers and informing people through snail-mail. But the Internet will always be tops when you are doing such recurrent marketing.

BJ STEPHENS

9
UNDERSTANDING WHAT YOU CAN AND CANNOT DO

Food for thought:

We all have rules we must live by and the sales profession there are some common sense ones, which you must keep in mind at all times. A good rule of thumb is to remember that your integrity, your business, your livelihood in on the line and if it feels uncomfortable or doesn't make sense then just don't do it.

Most of this book is about the fact that you can sell anything you want and how to go about doing just that but the real question is, "Can you sell *anything*?" Apply your common sense and get real. By knowing what you shouldn't sell then you brand yourself with one of the highest skills in the profession – honesty! This can work in your favor and put you at the top of the class but you must fully understand that the slightest wrinkle in your application of these "do's and don'ts" will be far more harmful than if you did nothing at all.

Below are just some of the rules you need to apply:

Illegal Stuff

This should go without saying yet many times every day you will come across someone who is not only bending the rules but are actually flaunting the fact. These are definitely stupid people. The risks that they take (and I will also include those that _buy_ from these unscrupulous people) put not only the profession in a bad light but can in fact, ruin your reputation if you are in a similar company. For instance, if you are in the health and wellness industry and are selling natural products that are safe for consumption and a competitor comes along and starts selling another "similar" product but from a sleazy company who is only after the almighty dollar and they don't care about the consumer. You will be questioned over and over again about your product vs. what they are looking at from the other competitor's product. Now you are in the position to have to "prove" your products' value and worth compared to the other one and that will take up a lot of time on your part and could, as an end result, get you into a position that makes your company look "more expensive", or not valuable enough in the customer's eyes. That is why I mentioned earlier to spend time knowing everything about your product so when you are inadvertently placed in a comparison situation you are fully armed with the best information and you actually can compete with those other companies on a knowledge basis, not an income basis.

If you are new to this profession or someone who wants to pursue the possibility then please, please, please do your homework and seek out only those with solid reputations. You can always check with the Better Business Bureaus of your area for a start. They will have reports available for viewing regarding any complaints from consumers. You can also check with your local Chamber of Commerce office and when in doubt, Google your inquiry but a word of caution here. If you Google, make sure that you read ALL comments, not just the ones you think look good and are favorable. Arm yourself with all the information you can so that you can make the best-informed decision.

And remember, if it sounds too good to be true, it usually is. Use your gut, your head and your common sense. This cannot be stressed enough.

Plagiarized Stuff

This should be common sense, yet again, every day, someone wants to test these boundaries. They do not want to put in the effort to do something that is uniquely theirs, that sets them out from the rest.

I will make a slight variance here however. There are things called PLR's, MRR's, RR's (Private Label Rights, Master Resale Rights, Resale Rights) and Personal

Use/Developer Rights. These are articles, video's, books, etc. that can be remade, re-written and reconfigured, for the most part, to be authentically yours. In some cases, you have the right to edit, claim as your own, resale and so forth, but each comes with a specific license and if you use them make sure that you understand exactly what the license covers. For someone who is just starting out and wants to establish a brand of his or her own this isn't a bad place to start. But the word of caution is inserted here. Make sure that you make enough revisions, write in your OWN voice, and insert enough changes that you are indeed the author. DO NOT copy word for word and just put your moniker on it. That is indeed plagiarizing and you are welcoming in a whole world of hurt.

Don't become a "drifter"

Now I want to address a fact that is a real problem in Network Marketing and literally makes me sick at my stomach when I see it happening.

Don't become a "drifter", someone who goes from company to company looking for the better compensation plan or the better rewards. That is not flattering to you whatsoever. Do your homework, find a company that you can get behind, believe in and offer to customers with pride. Now having said that, I am fully aware that if you are new to this profession it is harder to pick one company from the get-go and know everything about it. That is where doing your homework will pay off. There are many solid companies out there with excellent reputations and offer the public good products and good value to their affiliates, but there are many who are not. If you find yourself not happy with the particular company you are with then by all means find another but avoid trying to work two or three of them at the same time. Again, please take advise from someone who has done that and has failed miserably. It doesn't work. That is why before you spend your hard earned money and invest time and effort into your new company, find one that you know you are comfortable with from the start. Spreading yourself too thin will never, never work.

BJ STEPHENS

10 *THERE'S NO SUCH THING AS PERFECT BUT YOU CAN BECOME BETTER BY FAILURES*

FOOD FOR THOUGHT:

ASK YOURSELF IF WHAT YOU ARE DOING TODAY IS GETTING YOU CLOSER TO WHERE YOU WANT TO BE TOMORROW?

In spite of your best intentions and efforts no one is ever going to sell to every person they come in contact with. The best thing you can do for yourself is not to take the rejections personally and for the beginner this is hard to overcome. Remember what I said in the early part of this book? No doesn't always mean a permanent no; it could mean not right now. No may mean it's just not the right time because of money constraints for your customer, or perhaps something is going on in their personal life, or any other of a plethora of reasons. I always ask you to put yourself in the customer's shoes. Remember back to a time when someone approached you and asked you to make a purchase and you said no. What was your reason? Did that keep you from EVER purchasing the product? Probably not and you need to be mindful of their reasons. Don't give up forever on that customer. Instead put them on your future contact list and call on them again in the future. If you get a second or third no, then that's when you could probably should cut your loses.

Failure is a learning tool, not a permanent fixture in your life. The more you try and work on your techniques to sell things, the more you learn, grow and prosper. You learn what works and what doesn't. You learn what type of customer you can sell to and what type you can't and that is a HUGE lesson. You are going to learn that you click right away with certain personalities right off the bat and you will also learn that there are personalities that you would prefer to avoid at all costs. You learn who will keep buying from you and who will just be a drifter, you know, the "tire kickers". You will learn what you must do to open the dialog and how to maximize your skills to make that sale stick. Until those lessons are learned you will keep making those mistakes over and over. Guaranteed. There is absolutely no shame in failing and I always have chosen to see it as a measuring stick because if you are not failing then you are not learning and growing.

It is important that you do not let your failures bog you down and misdirect you from your goals. If you couldn't sell something to someone this time, then perhaps next time you can try a different approach. Do a self-critique but do not be overly harsh with yourself. Ask yourself, Did I come across too pushy? Did I falter on my rebuttal responses? Was I too quick with my answers? Did I come across as uninformed or unprofessional? Did I bring a fair representation of my samples and product? Could I have improved on my communication skill? These are always good questions to ask and not just for the "newbie". Seasoned professionals should be doing this as well following each and every sale. That is how we grow and get better.

Remember these points:

1. There is no guarantee that a person will buy from you, regardless of the efforts you put into making the sale. However, you can always increase the chances of them buying your product. You can do this by getting to know and understand their likes and dislikes and making your product more attractive for them.

2. Remember that your product won't have staying power, no matter what kind of product it is. Some products are fads, some products are replaced the net year by a "new and improved formula", and so forth. It is for that reason you need to keep improving your creativeness by bringing new versions, updates and samples. Make sure that you have the most current product and let your customers know that right up front in your presentation.

3. Every failed sale teaches you something. Use those failures as a learning tool. Self-improvement is one sure way to guarantee more sales for your future and lends to your professional image.
4. Always keep a lookout on how other people are marketing their stuff. In fact, I strongly urge you to buy your competition's merchandise or attend those business fairs. Pick up flyers and brochures and check out how they are targeting their audiences. See for yourself what convinced people to buy from them.
5. Keep improving. Keep learning. Keep educating yourself. Keep evolving. Keep investing in yourself! You will become a better salesperson tomorrow than you are today just because you kept trying.

BONUS: INVEST IN A COACH AND MENTOR – THE EXTREME VALUE IN INVESTING IN YOURSELF

Food for thought

"A lot of people have gone further than they ever thought because someone else thought they could and helped them through the tough times and struggles. A good mentor will push you to those levels that you don't believe are possible."

*-Anonymous_*

No one can manage success all by themselves

I do not know where I honestly would be if it were not for the fabulous mentors and coaches that I have been blessed with throughout my career. These loving, supportive, generous, and extremely wise men have all helped push me to the levels that I never thought were possible.

I wished I could convey more eloquently how extremely important this step is in your career – regardless of what that career is. There are so many intricacies into becoming successful and sometimes we just need that gentle nudge to keep our spirits high, or to help us keep focused when things are a struggle in our every day lives. Sometimes, because we allow so much negative self-talk to influence our daily actions (which leads to a ton of self-doubt and a lack of confidence!), we need that "voice of reasonability" to help us on track.

These are people you should be diligent in seeking out; don't just go with the "popular" ones, the ones who make outrageous promises and then because you can't pay their ungodly fees leave you hanging in the breeze. You do need to ask friends, co-workers, people you trust for recommendations and then do your homework. Just because one mentor/coach worked for someone else DOES NOT mean they are the right fit for you! That's one of the biggest mistakes most people make right out of the gate.

I strongly suggest you schedule a talk with your choices and have a list of questions already written down that you ask each one of them. Based on their conversation, make a choice that you are the most comfortable with. View their videos, check them out on YouTube, follow a group of theirs on Facebook, etc. Research each one out thoroughly!

And let's talk fees. Oh my gosh! I wish I could spend pages on this because it is my humble opinion a really good coach and mentor shouldn't cost you an arm and a leg or your child's college fund! Let me make this as clear as I can possibly be. Yes, you will have to spend money and sometimes you will spend that money over a period of time but don't subscribe to something that costs $5000 and takes only 3 months to complete. ABSOLUTELY NOT!!!!!

There are many good and more than qualified coaches/mentors out their who give you personalized 1-1 attention and training and are sincerely committed to YOUR goals, not theirs! It is one of the main reasons that I got into the coaching/mentoring/training profession myself. I desperately needed the advice and counsel of mentorship but because I was working a full time job (no, scratch that. I was working 3 jobs at one time just to make ends meet!) I didn't have a ton of money that I could spend on coaching so I got deeply frustrated.

Coaching/Mentoring is of course a business, first and foremost, without question, and yes, these people have the same kind of obligations that you have as well, but a **true** coach/mentor will be flexible, reasonable, and understanding (or should be in my book!) and will try and work with you. Now, that isn't to say that everyone will and many of them may tell you no. Don't worry or fret, just keep searching because I promise you there are people out there, there is someone who is the ideal mentor for you.

One more important thing to consider. Don't just settle on

one particular **type** of coach/mentor. In your path to success and true entrepreneurism you will need to invest in several. That, too, is just a fact of life. Success cannot and will not happen unless you have the help of several who can guide you to that dream. I have had no less than six and yes, some of them cost me a huge chunk of change, but remember what I said in the beginning? You are the most important investment you will ever make and honestly, your future depends, in part, on how much you consider you to be worth.

At the end of this book I share with you some of the KEY mentors in my career and unfortunately, two of the best are no longer residing on this earth and I will also admit that I grieved sadly over their passing. They became indispensable to me and my success and I would definitely not be where I am today without them. That is the kind of mentor/coach you need to seek out. Be patient with the process, don't rush it. After all, this you do for YOU, the most valuable asset you own!

"YOU CAN EVERYTHING YOU WANT WHEN YOU LEARN TO GIVE EVERYONE ELSE WHAT THEY WANT" – Zig Ziglar

ABOUT THE AUTHOR

After a varied work career including fields such as law enforcement, insurance, health care, education, retail and manufacturing, BJ chose to pursue a full time career as a public speaker, speaker and presentation coach, and leadership consulting. BJ has also spent over fifty years in direct sales and marketing. She has also spent several years as a teacher, trainer and coach for both individual professionals and small business companies.

She has been trained and mentored by some of the industry giants and legends including Zig Ziglar, Jim Rohn, Les Brown, John Maxwell and so many others and it is to these individuals that she proudly states that much of her success has come to her through their loving patience, guidance, and barrels of support.

BJ is also a proud member of Toastmasters International where she currently holds the distinctive certifications of ALB, ACS, but also served as an Area Director for six other clubs providing leadership, mentorship and guidance to ensure their success as individual clubs. Her ultimate goal will be to achieve the highest award Toastmasters offers, ACP (Accredited Certified Speaker).

She also a proud member of the The John Maxwell Team and will be earning her certification as a certified speaker/coach/trainer sometime in 2018.

BJ and her long time partner of twenty five years, Kevin, live in SE Iowa where they enjoy traveling, checking out new and different dining experiences (that includes that Diner, Drive-Ins, and Dives experience) and their six cats, Ozzie, Boo, Groucho, Tinker, Butterz, and Ollie.

www.ingramcontent.com/pod-product-compliance
Lightning Source LLC
Chambersburg PA
CBHW040233220526
45473CB00001B/224